AMAZING MOMENTS

Super Bowl COMEBACK!

Tom Brady and the Patriots at Super Bowl LI

By Mark and Solomon Shulman
Illustrated by Chris Fowler

BEARPORT PUBLISHING
Minneapolis, Minnesota
BEAR CLAW

Credits

Cover art by Tom Rogers. Photos: 20: © Dean Bertoncelj/Dreamstime; 21T: © Tony Tomsic/AP Photos; 21B: © Rich Graessle/Icon Sportwire/Newscom. 22: Ric Tapia/Icon Sportswire/Newscom; 23: © Jerry Coli/Dreamstime.

Bearport Publishing Company Product Development Team
President: Jen Jenson; Director of Product Development: Spencer Brinker; Managing Editor: Allison Juda; Associate Editor: Naomi Reich; Senior Designer: Colin O'Dea; Associate Designer: Elena Klinkner; Associate Designer: Kayla Eggert; Product Development Specialist: Anita Stasson

Produced by Shoreline Publishing Group LLC
Santa Barbara, California
Designer: Patty Kelley
Editorial Director: James Buckley Jr.

DISCLAIMER: This graphic story is a dramatization based on true events. It is intended to give the reader a sense of the narrative rather than a presentation of actual details as they occurred.

Library of Congress Cataloging-in-Publication Data

Names: Shulman, Mark, 1962- author. | Shulman, Solomon, author. | Fowler,
   Chris illustrator.
Title: Super Bowl comeback! : Tom Brady and the Patriots at Super Bowl LI /
   by Mark and Solomon Shulman ; illustrated by Chris Fowler.
Description: Minneapolis, MN : Bearport Publishing Company, [2024] |
   Series: Amazing moments in sports | Includes bibliographical references
   and index.
Identifiers: LCCN 2023005600 (print) | LCCN 2023005601 (ebook) | ISBN
   9798885099905 (library binding) | ISBN 9798888221723 (paperback) | ISBN
   9798888223055 (ebook)
Subjects: LCSH: New England Patriots (Football team)--Juvenile literature.
   | Brady, Tom, 1977---Juvenile literature. | Super Bowl (51st : 2017 :
   Houston, Tex.)--Juvenile literature.
Classification: LCC GV956.N36 S58 2024 (print) | LCC GV956.N36 (ebook) |
   DDC 796.332092 [B]--dc23/eng/20230213
LC record available at https://lccn.loc.gov/2023005600
LC ebook record available at https://lccn.loc.gov/2023005601

For more information, write to Bearport Publishing, 5357 Penn Avenue South, Minneapolis, MN 55419.

CONTENTS

Chapter 1

SUPER BOWL BLOWOUT

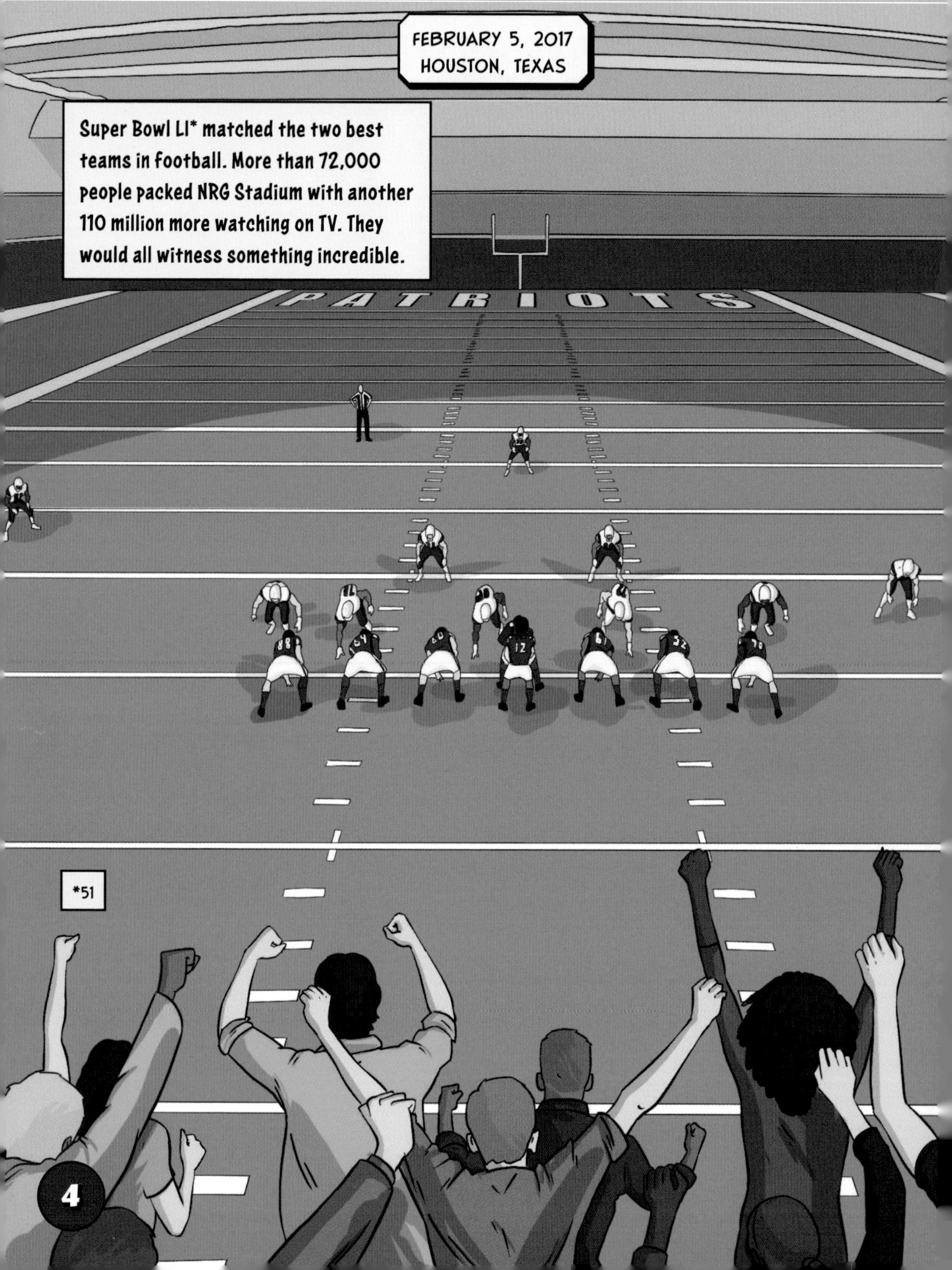
FEBRUARY 5, 2017
HOUSTON, TEXAS
Super Bowl LI* matched the two best teams in football. More than 72,000 people packed NRG Stadium with another 110 million more watching on TV. They would all witness something incredible.
PATRIOTS
*51

Quarterback Matt Ryan led the Atlanta Falcons. The team was making its second Super Bowl appearance.

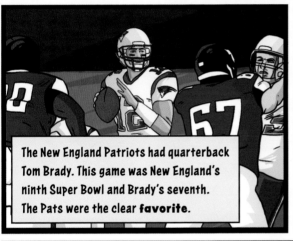

The New England Patriots had quarterback Tom Brady. This game was New England's ninth Super Bowl and Brady's seventh. The Pats were the clear **favorite**.

However, with only 21 minutes remaining, a Patriots win *didn't* seem likely! The Falcons led 28-3.

Still, Brady had four Super Bowl victories in his great career. He was not the kind to quit!

LET'S TURN THIS GAME AROUND!

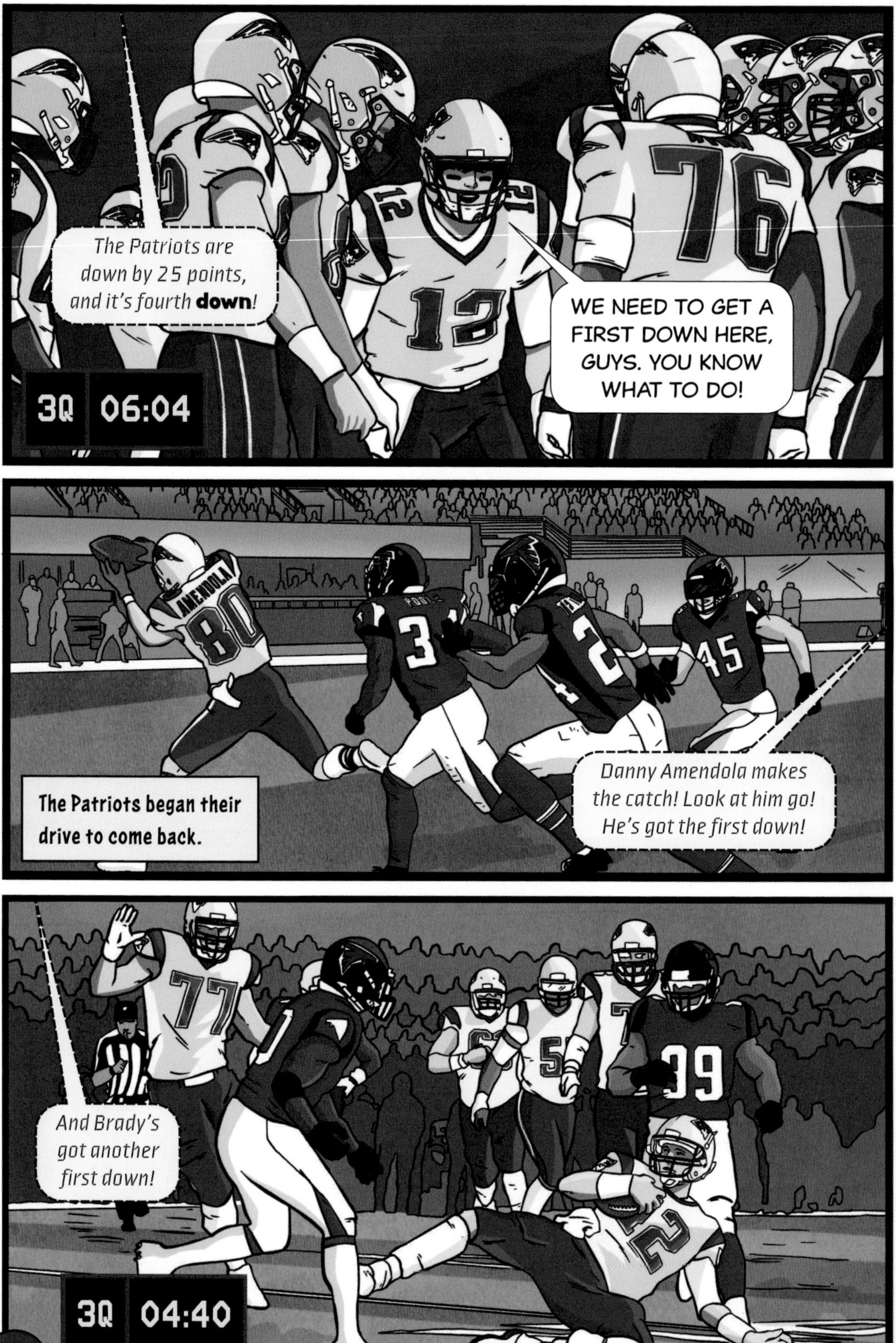
3Q 06:04
The Patriots are down by 25 points, and it's fourth **down**!
WE NEED TO GET A FIRST DOWN HERE, GUYS. YOU KNOW WHAT TO DO!
The Patriots began their drive to come back.
Danny Amendola makes the catch! Look at him go! He's got the first down!
And Brady's got another first down!
3Q 04:40

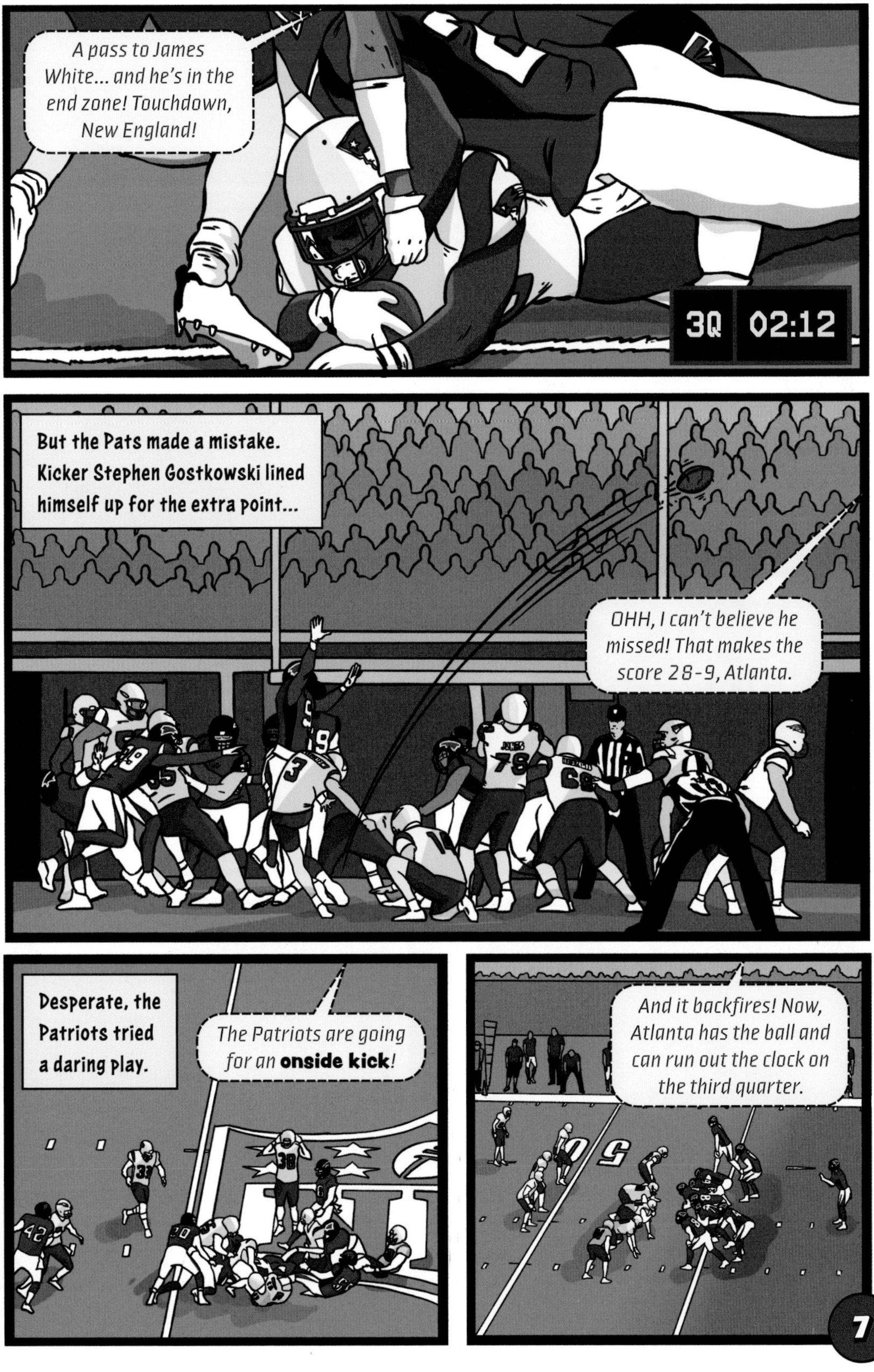
A pass to James White... and he's in the end zone! Touchdown, New England!
3Q
02:12
But the Pats made a mistake. Kicker Stephen Gostkowski lined himself up for the extra point...
OHH, I can't believe he missed! That makes the score 28-9, Atlanta.
Desperate, the Patriots tried a daring play.
The Patriots are going for an **onside kick**!
And it backfires! Now, Atlanta has the ball and can run out the clock on the third quarter.

Chapter 2

PATRIOTS RALLY

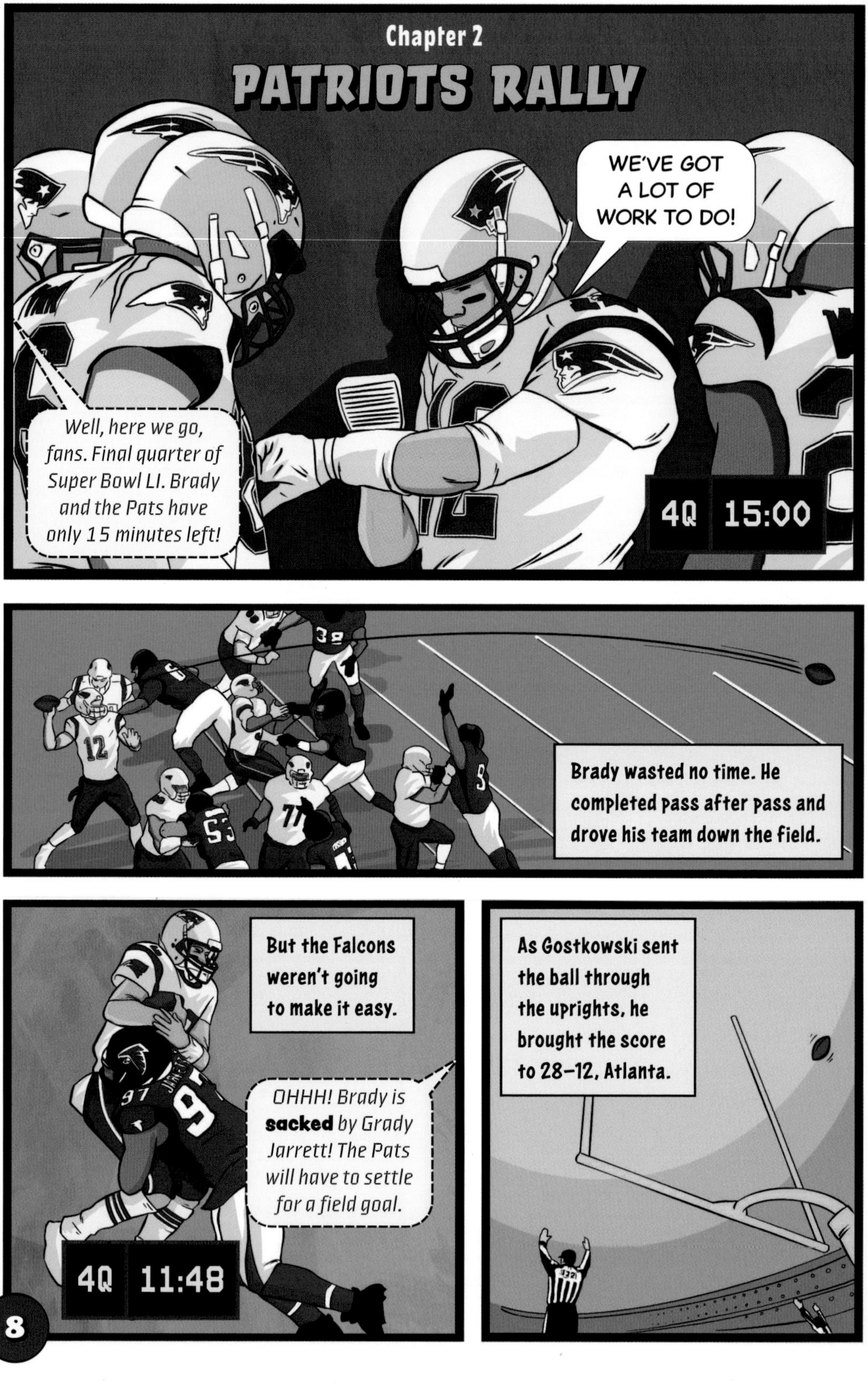
WE'VE GOT A LOT OF WORK TO DO!
Well, here we go, fans. Final quarter of Super Bowl LI. Brady and the Pats have only 15 minutes left!
4Q 15:00
Brady wasted no time. He completed pass after pass and drove his team down the field.
But the Falcons weren't going to make it easy.
OHHH! Brady is **sacked** by Grady Jarrett! The Pats will have to settle for a field goal.
4Q 11:48
As Gostkowski sent the ball through the uprights, he brought the score to 28–12, Atlanta.

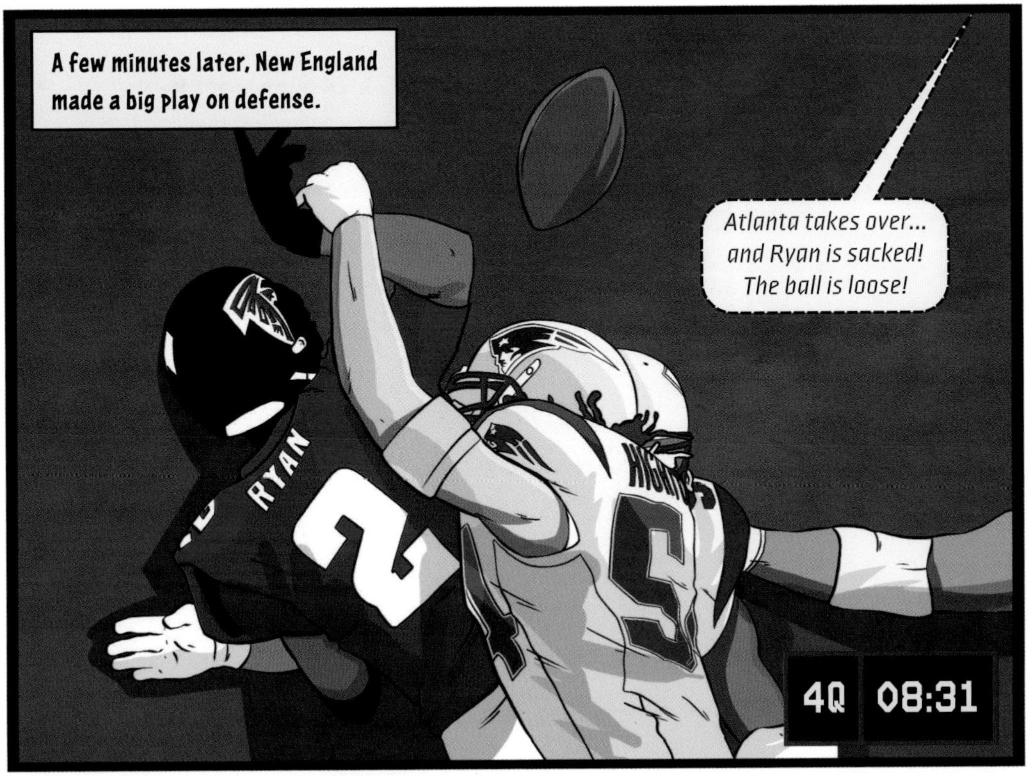
A few minutes later, New England made a big play on defense.
Atlanta takes over... and Ryan is sacked! The ball is loose!
RYAN
4Q 08:31

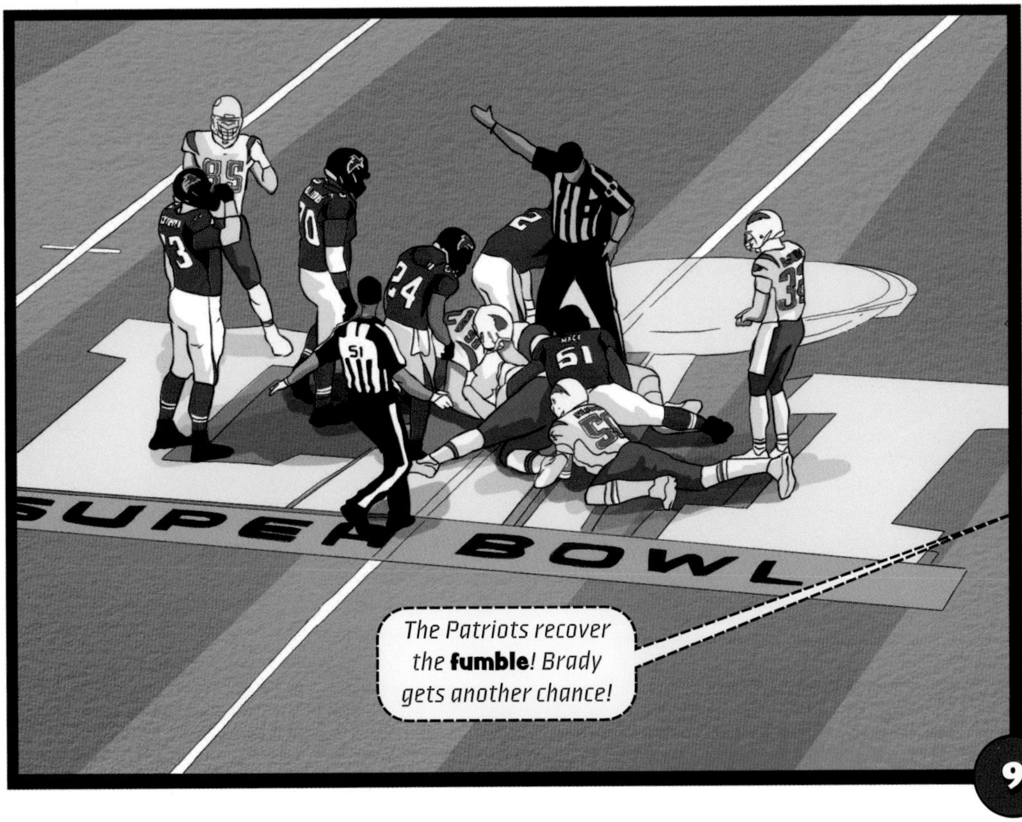
SUPER BOWL
The Patriots recover the **fumble**! Brady gets another chance!

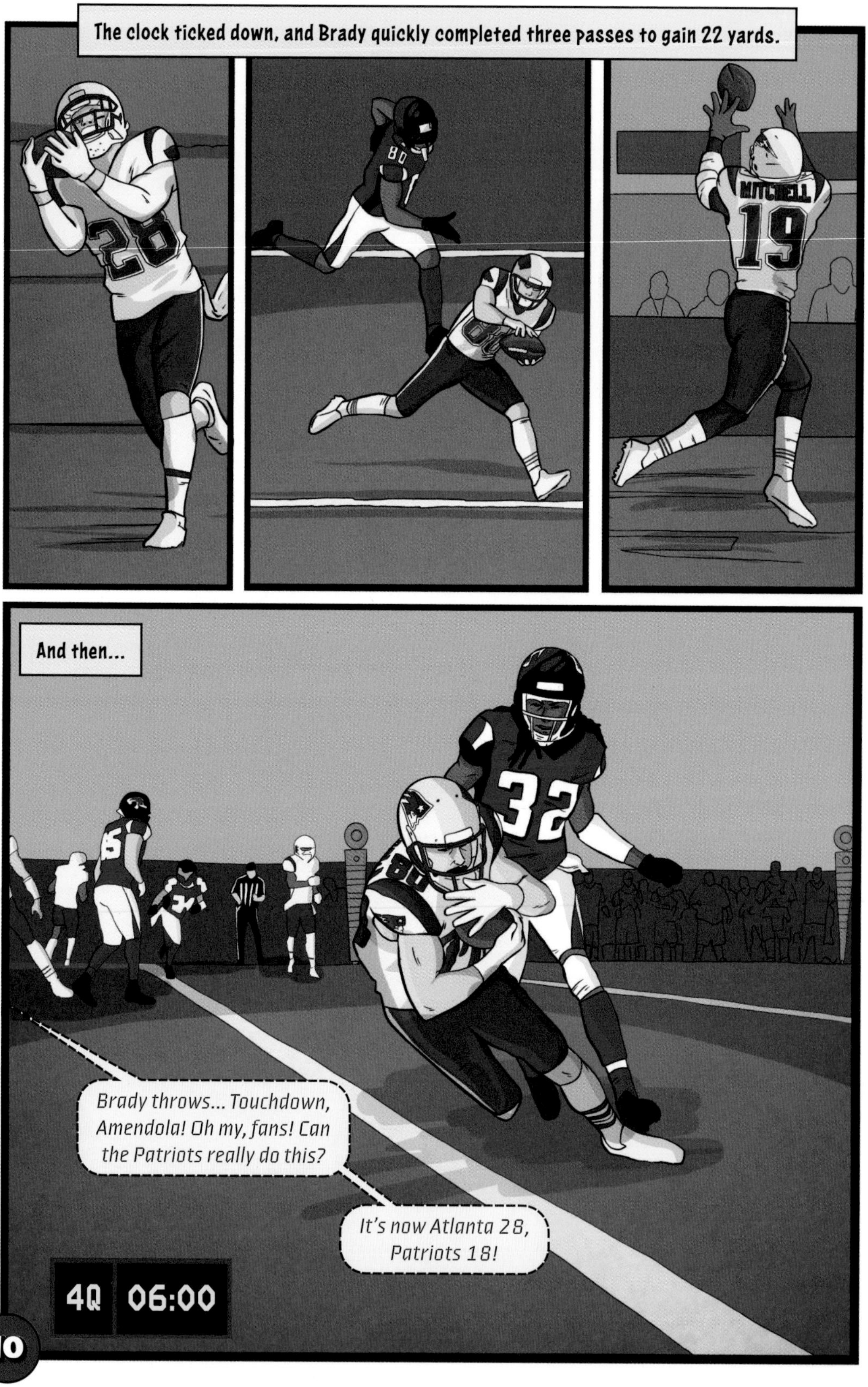
The clock ticked down, and Brady quickly completed three passes to gain 22 yards.
And then...
Brady throws... Touchdown, Amendola! Oh my, fans! Can the Patriots really do this?
It's now Atlanta 28, Patriots 18!
4Q 06:00

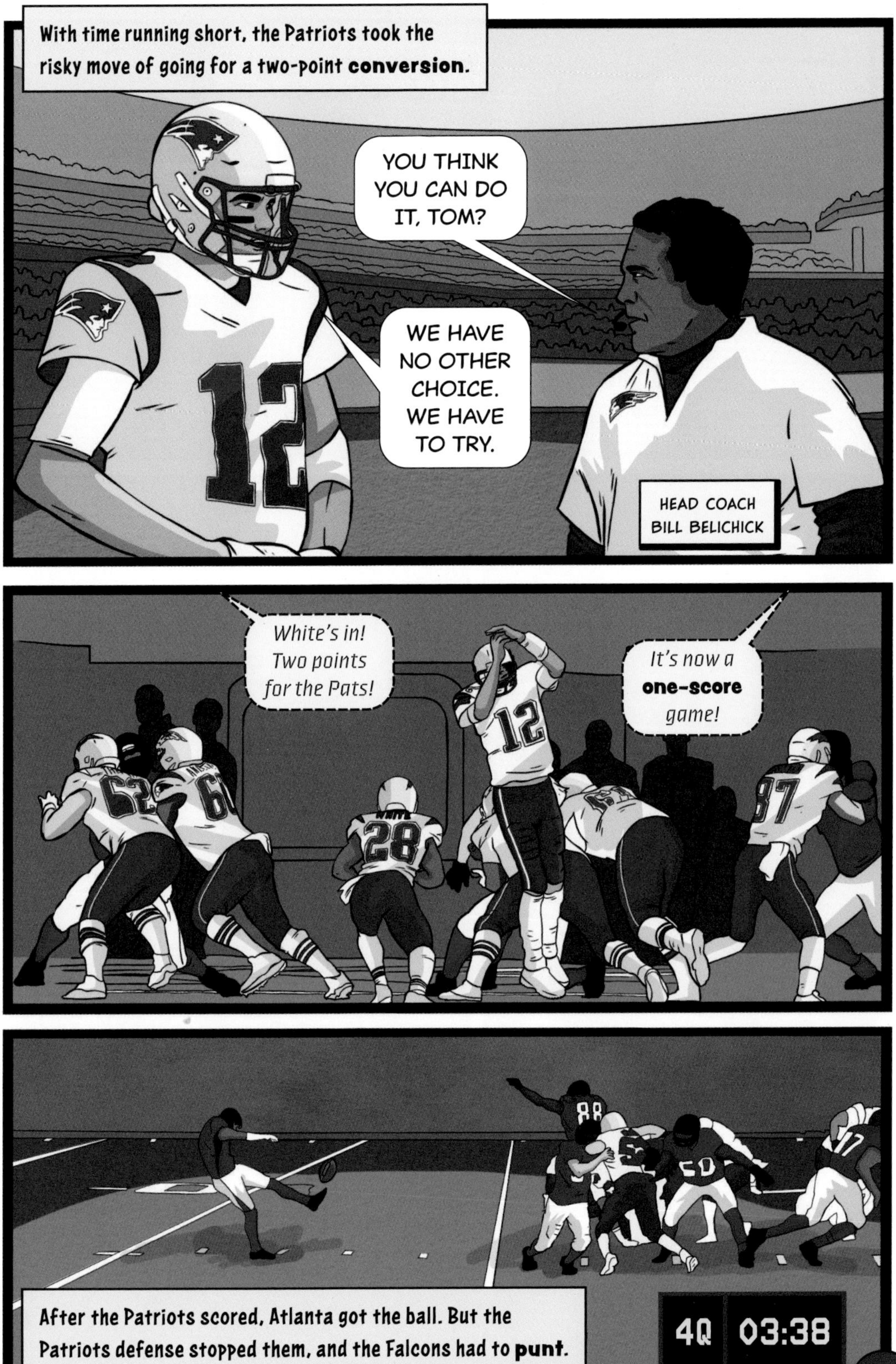
With time running short, the Patriots took the risky move of going for a two-point **conversion**.
YOU THINK YOU CAN DO IT, TOM?
WE HAVE NO OTHER CHOICE. WE HAVE TO TRY.
HEAD COACH BILL BELICHICK
White's in! Two points for the Pats!
It's now a **one-score** *game!*
After the Patriots scored, Atlanta got the ball. But the Patriots defense stopped them, and the Falcons had to **punt**.
4Q 03:38

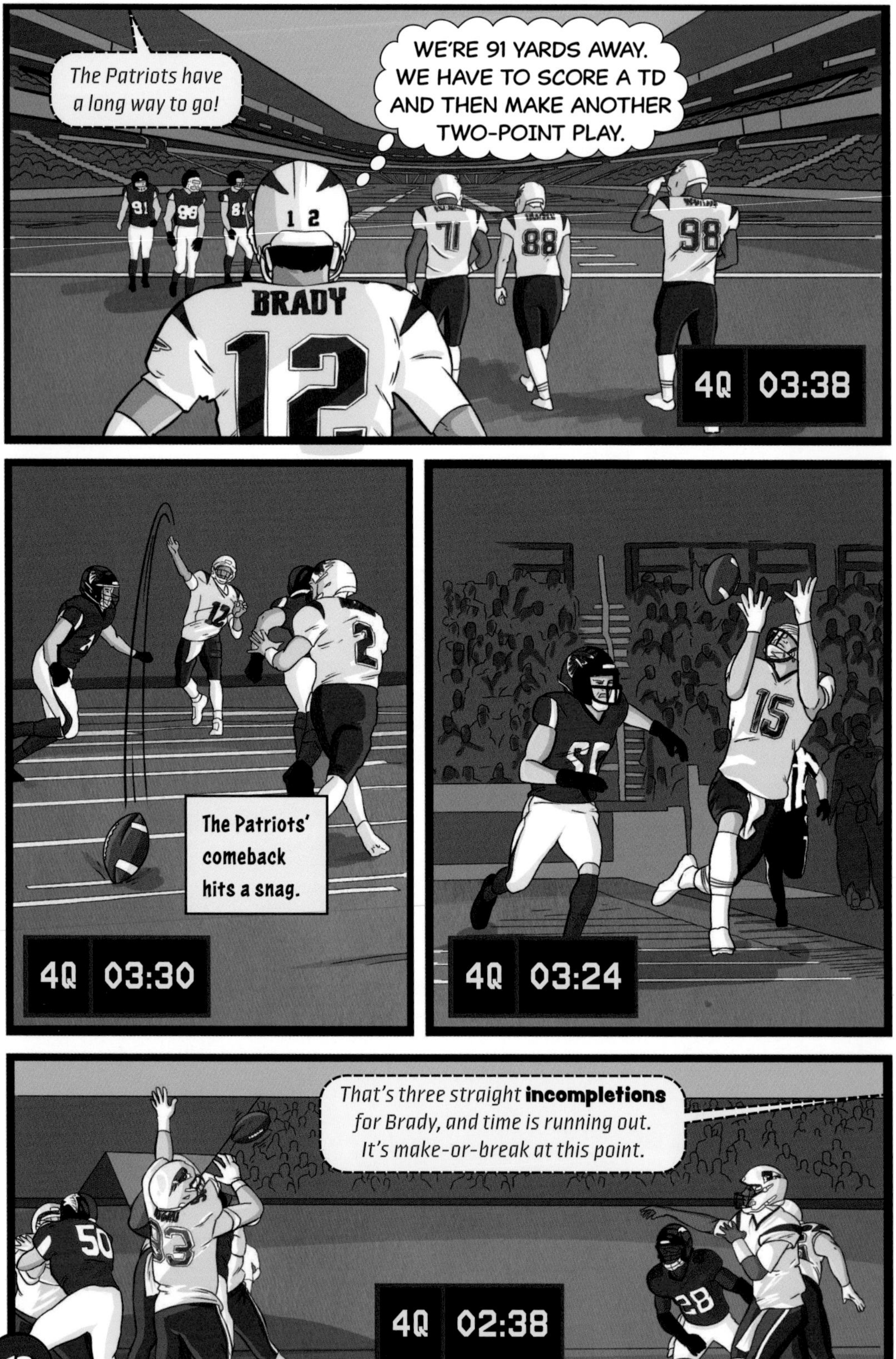
The Patriots have a long way to go!
WE'RE 91 YARDS AWAY. WE HAVE TO SCORE A TD AND THEN MAKE ANOTHER TWO-POINT PLAY.
BRADY
4Q 03:38
The Patriots' comeback hits a snag.
4Q 03:30
4Q 03:24
That's three straight **incompletions** for Brady, and time is running out. It's make-or-break at this point.
4Q 02:38

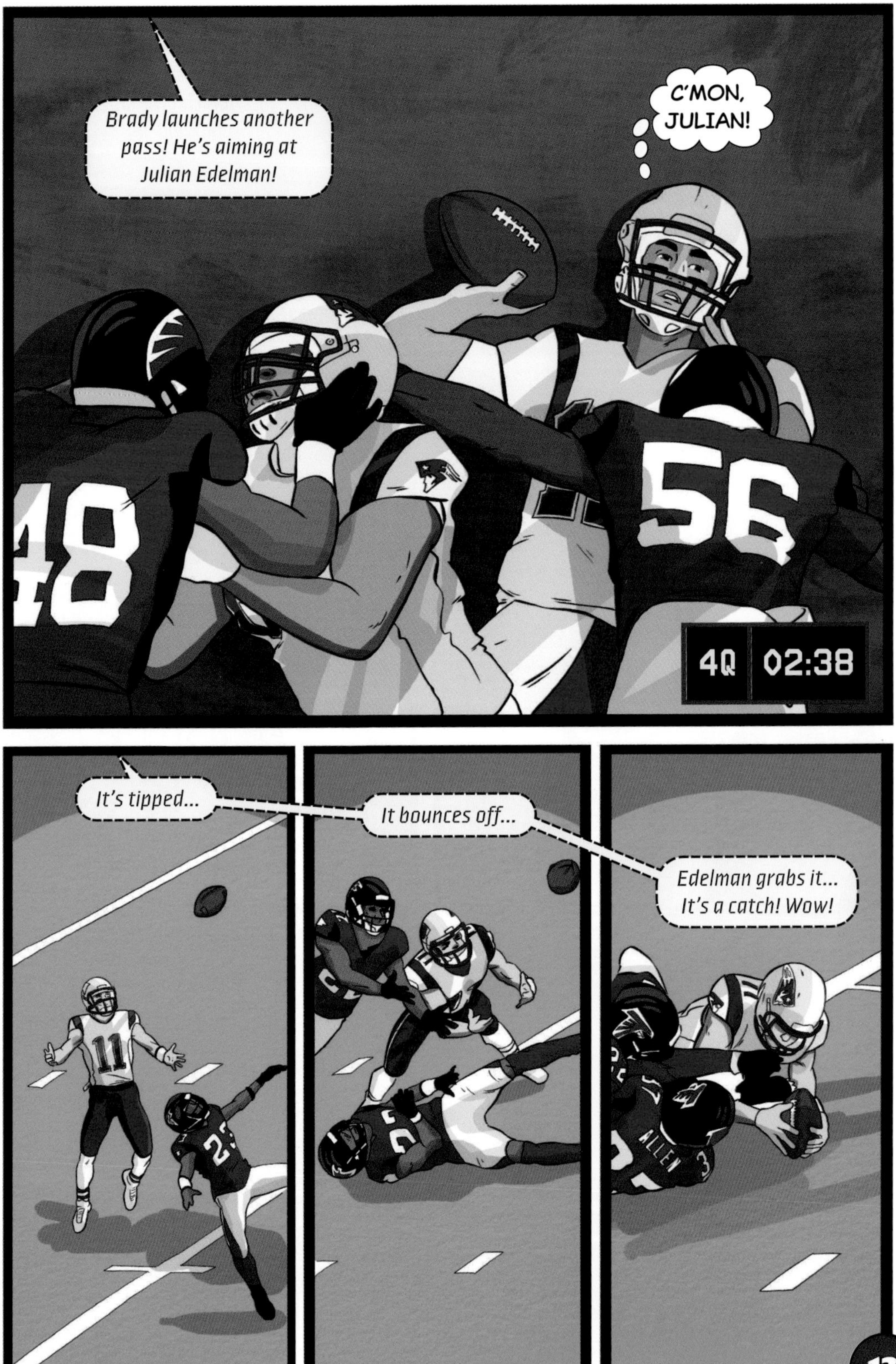

Brady launches another pass! He's aiming at Julian Edelman!
C'MON, JULIAN!
4Q 02:38
It's tipped...
It bounces off...
Edelman grabs it... It's a catch! Wow!

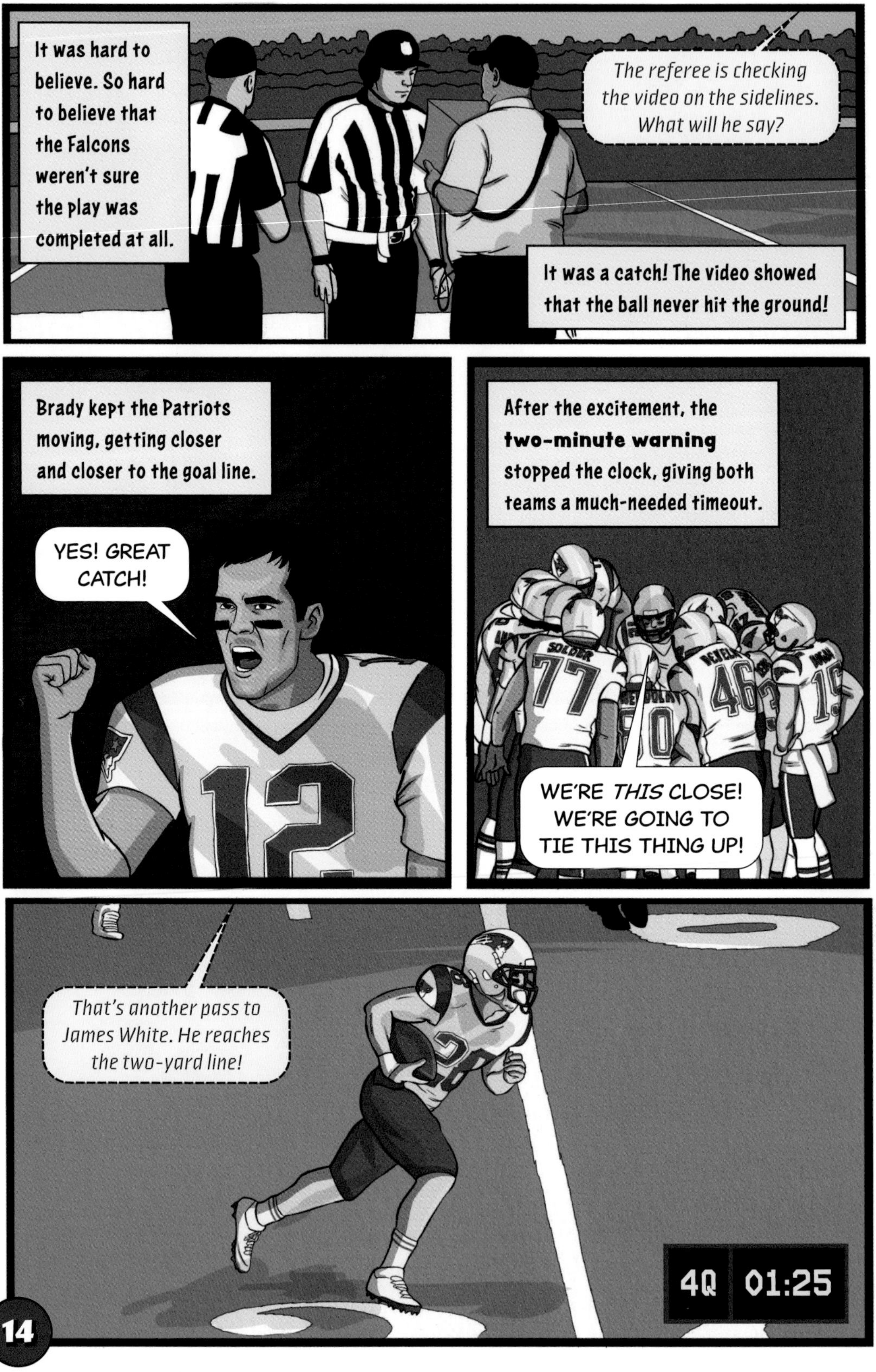
It was hard to believe. So hard to believe that the Falcons weren't sure the play was completed at all.
The referee is checking the video on the sidelines. What will he say?
It was a catch! The video showed that the ball never hit the ground!
Brady kept the Patriots moving, getting closer and closer to the goal line.
YES! GREAT CATCH!
After the excitement, the **two-minute warning** stopped the clock, giving both teams a much-needed timeout.
WE'RE *THIS* CLOSE! WE'RE GOING TO TIE THIS THING UP!
That's another pass to James White. He reaches the two-yard line!
4Q 01:25

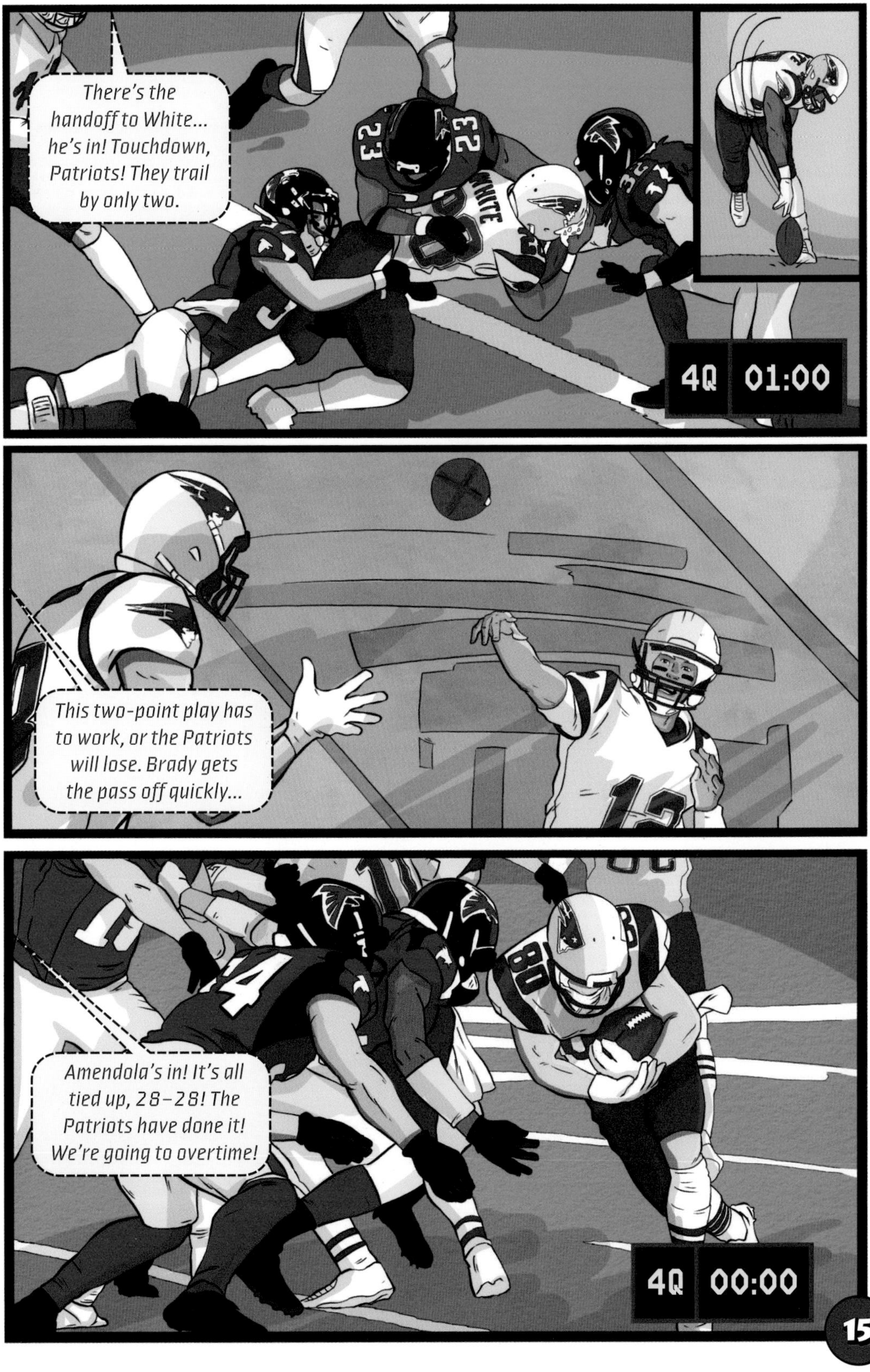
There's the handoff to White... he's in! Touchdown, Patriots! They trail by only two.
4Q 01:00
This two-point play has to work, or the Patriots will lose. Brady gets the pass off quickly...
Amendola's in! It's all tied up, 28–28! The Patriots have done it! We're going to overtime!
4Q 00:00

Chapter 3

OVERTIME WINNER!

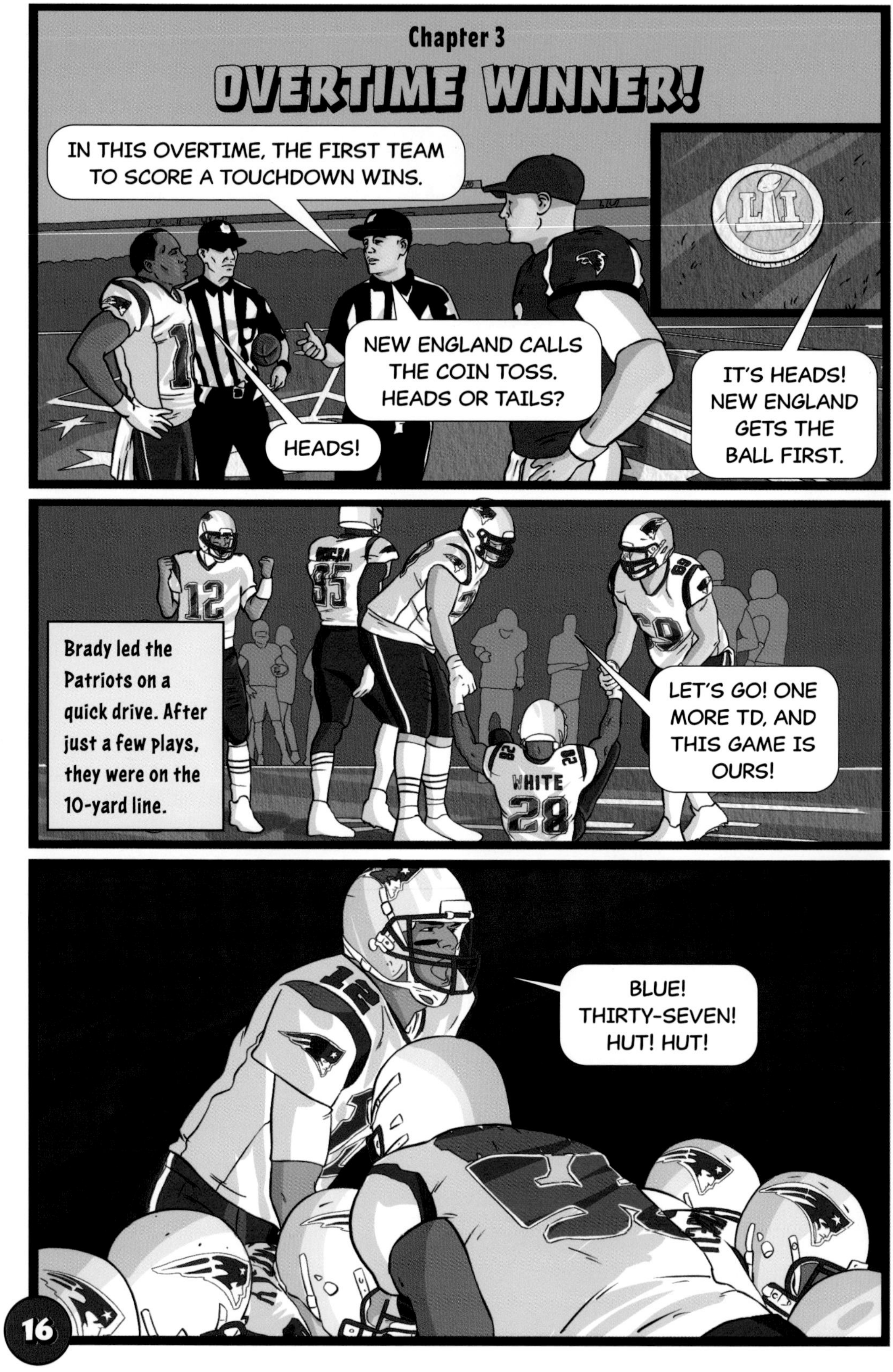
IN THIS OVERTIME, THE FIRST TEAM TO SCORE A TOUCHDOWN WINS.
NEW ENGLAND CALLS THE COIN TOSS. HEADS OR TAILS?
HEADS!
IT'S HEADS! NEW ENGLAND GETS THE BALL FIRST.
Brady led the Patriots on a quick drive. After just a few plays, they were on the 10-yard line.
LET'S GO! ONE MORE TD, AND THIS GAME IS OURS!
BLUE! THIRTY-SEVEN! HUT! HUT!

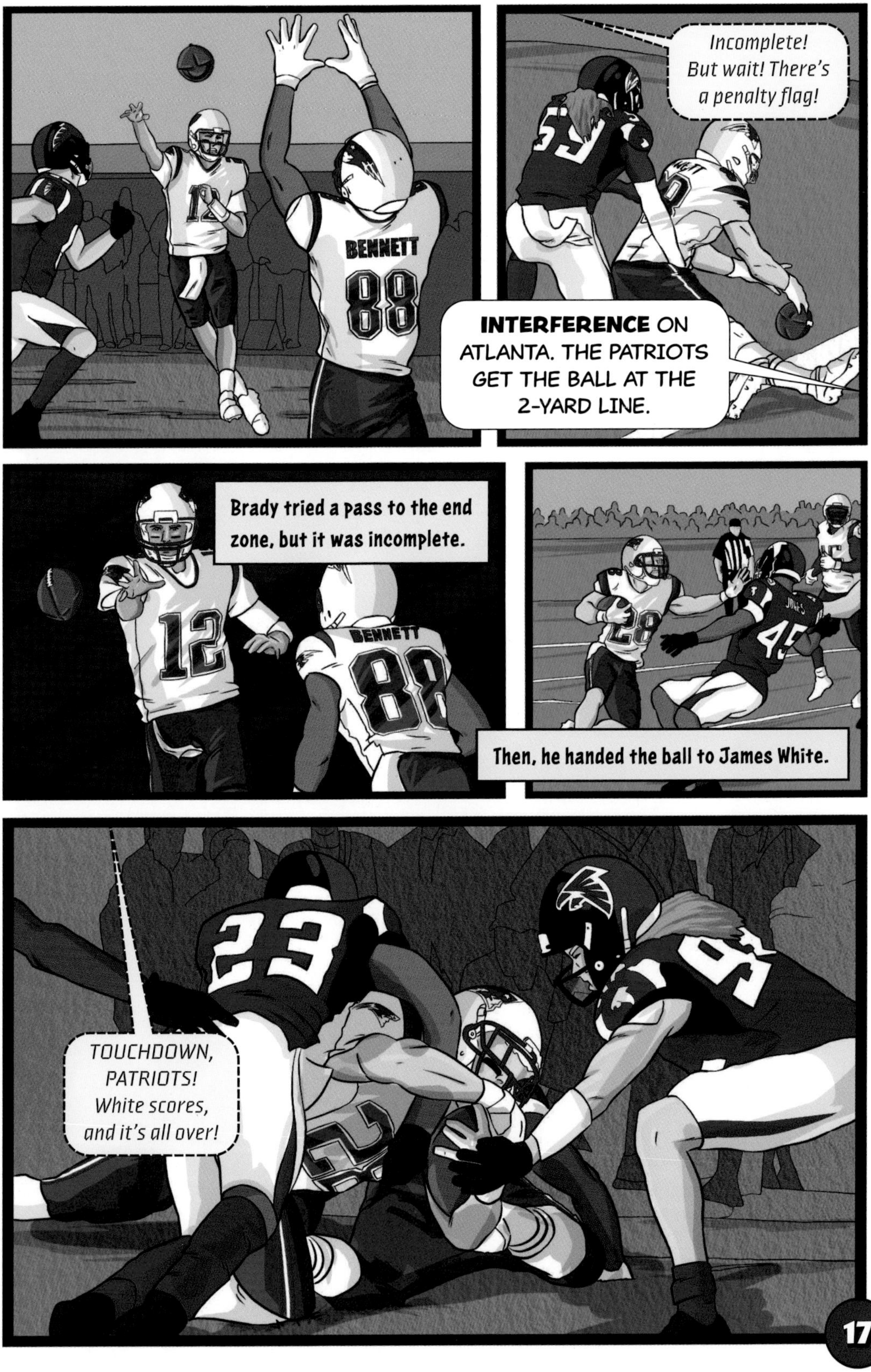
Incomplete! But wait! There's a penalty flag!
INTERFERENCE ON ATLANTA. THE PATRIOTS GET THE BALL AT THE 2-YARD LINE.
Brady tried a pass to the end zone, but it was incomplete.
Then, he handed the ball to James White.
TOUCHDOWN, PATRIOTS! White scores, and it's all over!

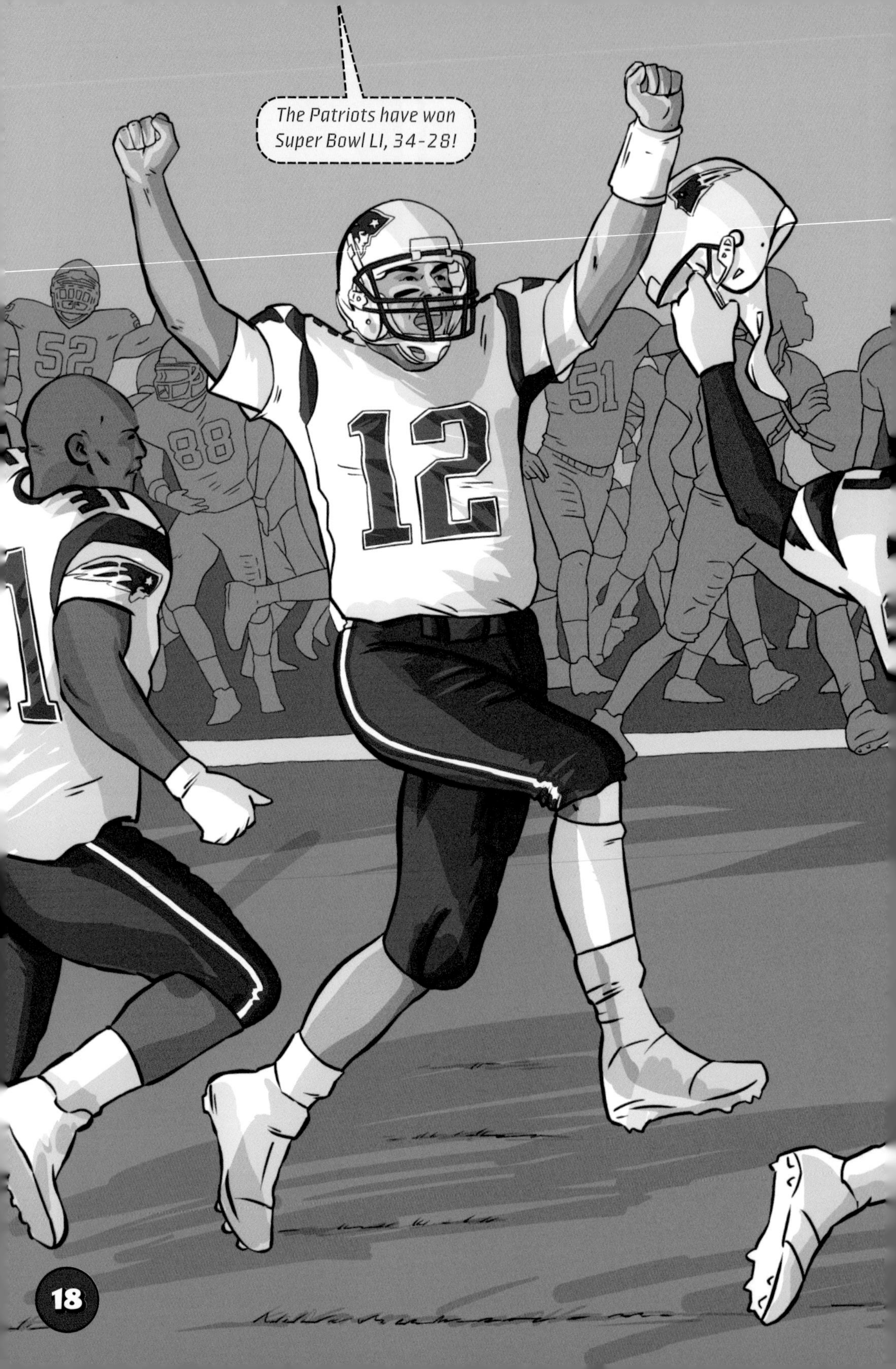
The Patriots have won Super Bowl LI, 34-28!

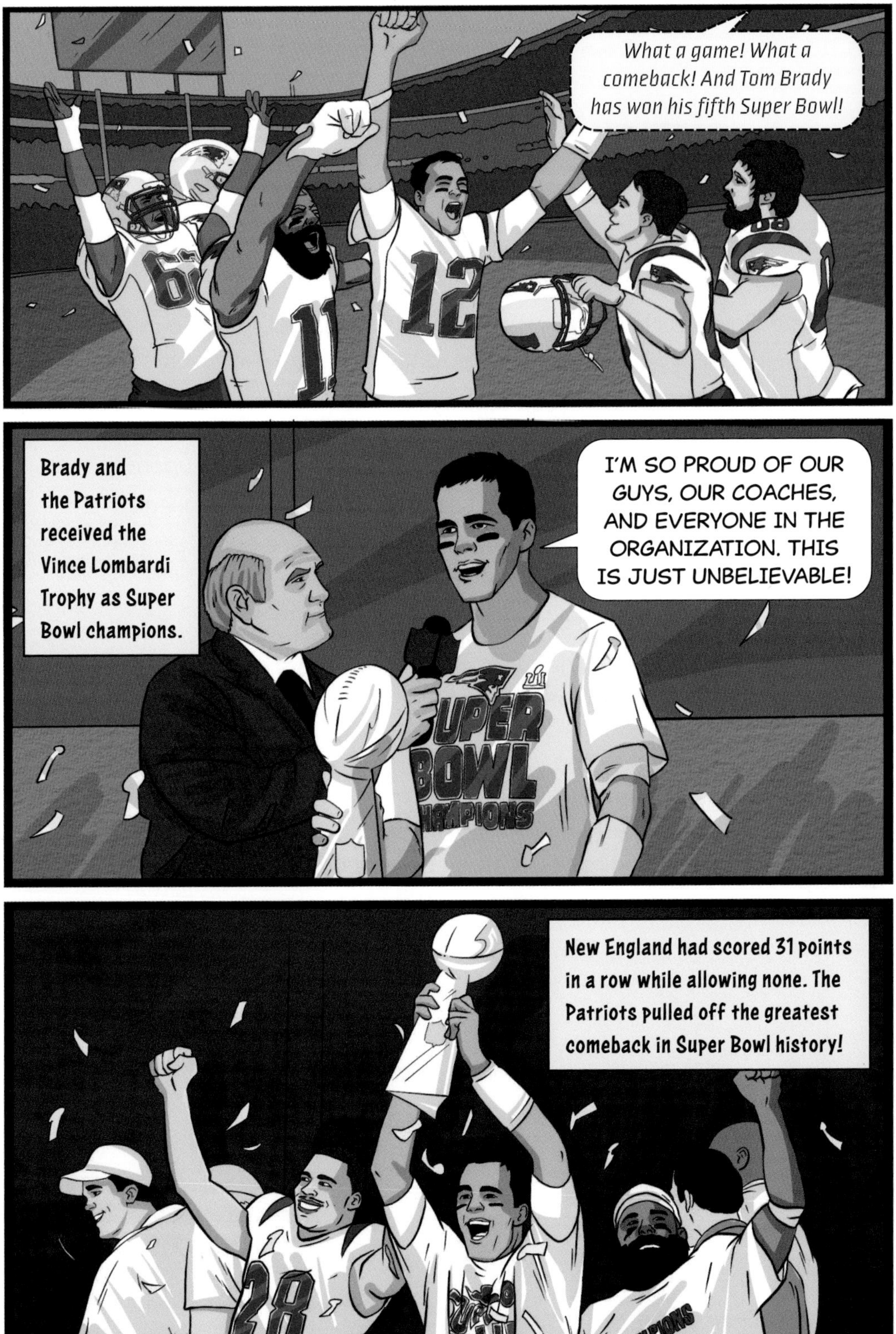
What a game! What a comeback! And Tom Brady has won his fifth Super Bowl!
Brady and the Patriots received the Vince Lombardi Trophy as Super Bowl champions.
I'M SO PROUD OF OUR GUYS, OUR COACHES, AND EVERYONE IN THE ORGANIZATION. THIS IS JUST UNBELIEVABLE!
SUPER BOWL CHAMPIONS
New England had scored 31 points in a row while allowing none. The Patriots pulled off the greatest comeback in Super Bowl history!

SUPER BOWL HISTORY

The first Super Bowl was played on January 15, 1967. In it, the Green Bay Packers beat the the Kansas City Chiefs, 35-10. Since then, the Super Bowl has become America's most-watched sporting event, complete with an elaborate halftime show. The game is held in a different stadium each year, usually in early February.

- The Super Bowl got its name from a toy called the Superball®. The word *bowl* was already used to describe some college football games and was swapped in to replace ball.
- Roman numerals were first used at Super Bowl V (5).
- Miami has hosted the most Super Bowls—six at Hard Rock Stadium and five at the Orange Bowl.
- More than 114 million people watched the Super Bowl in 2015. This was the biggest audience ever for a TV program.
- The Super Bowl halftime show has become almost as famous as the game. Superstar acts perform shows on the field.

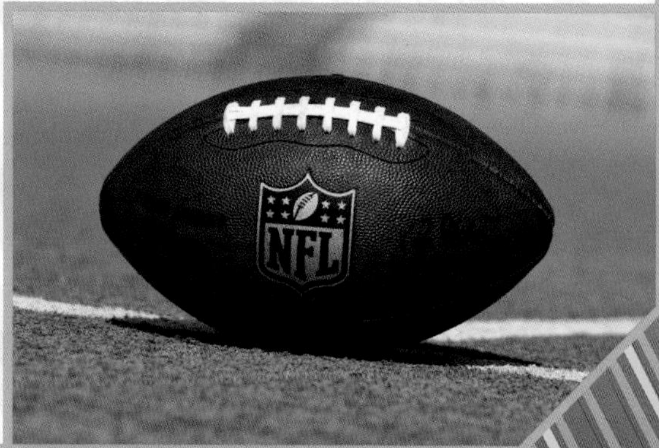
NFL

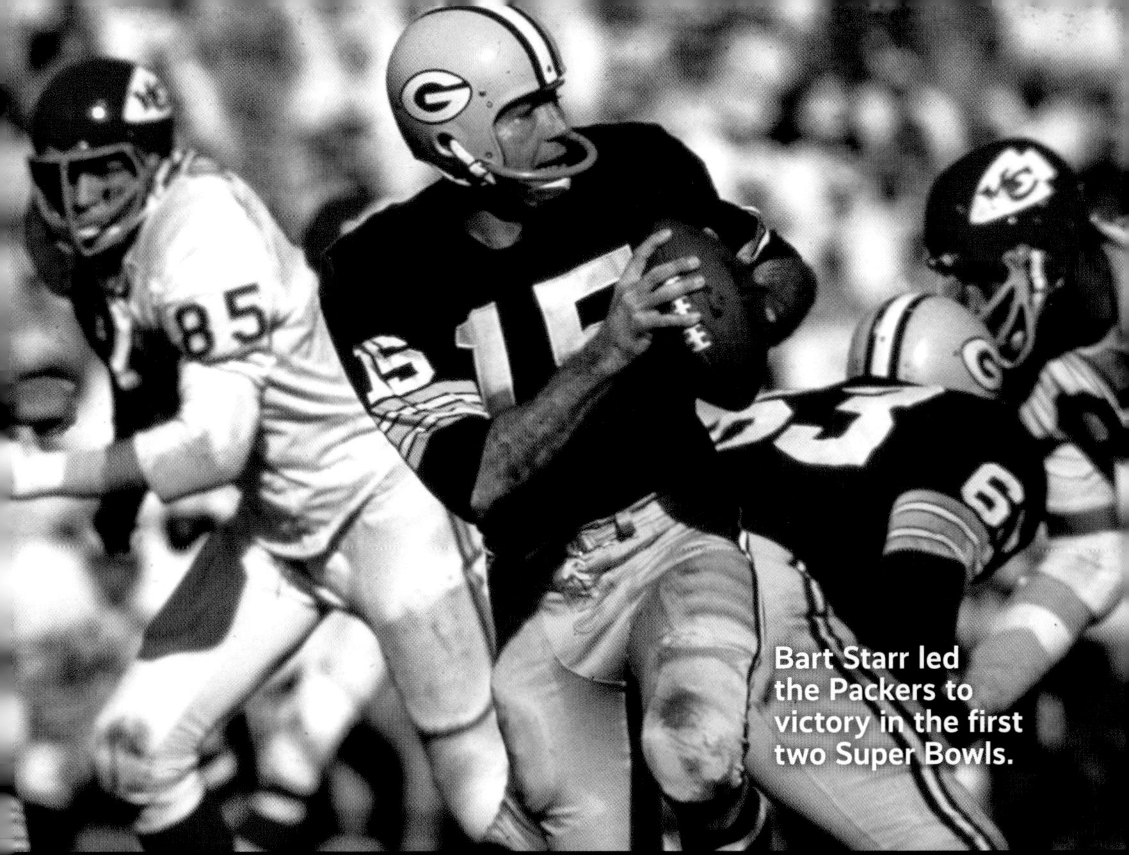

Bart Starr led the Packers to victory in the first two Super Bowls.

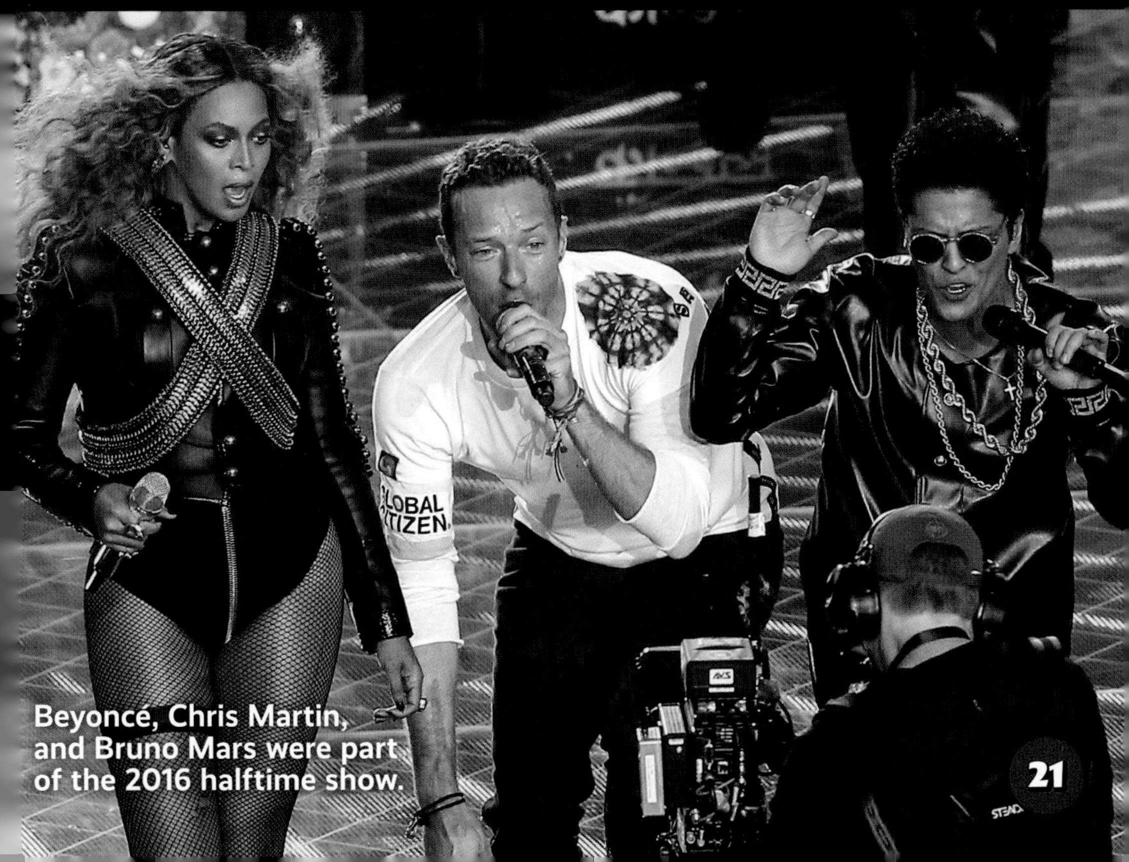

Beyoncé, Chris Martin, and Bruno Mars were part of the 2016 halftime show.

SUPER BOWL SUPER TEAMS

Four teams have won five or more Super Bowls.

Pittsburgh Steelers: The Steelers were the first team to win four Super Bowls. They were packed with Hall of Fame players in the 1970s. They made it six in all when they added two more titles with QB Ben Roethlisberger in the 2000s.

New England Patriots: QB Tom Brady and head coach Bill Belichick were a perfect team. They dominated the NFL for 20 seasons, winning six Super Bowls together.

San Francisco 49ers: QB Joe Montana and WR Jerry Rice were the key players for the Niners when they won four Super Bowls in the 1980s and early 90s. QB Steve Young led them to their fifth win in 1995.

Dallas Cowboys: After winning Super Bowls for the 1971 and 1977 seasons, the Cowboys didn't make it back to the top until QB Troy Aikman and RB Emmitt Smith led Dallas to three more titles in the 1990s.

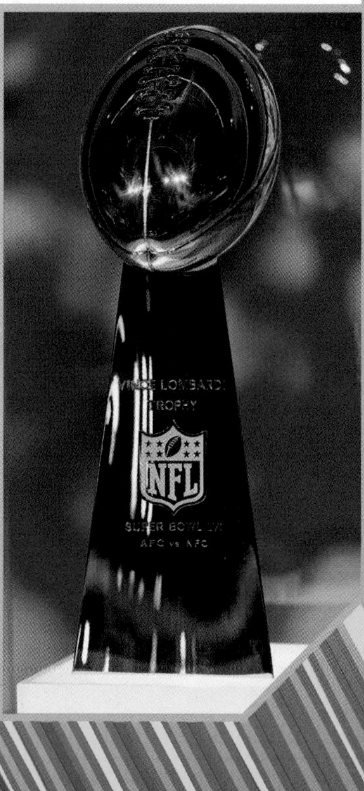
NFL

The Vince Lombardi Trophy is given to Super Bowl winning teams.

GLOSSARY

conversion a play run after a touchdown to add one or two points

down a single offensive play in football

favorite a team or player who is expected to win

fumble a ball that has been dropped

incompletions passes that are not caught

interference when one player stops another from catching a pass in a way that is against the rules

one-score a circumstance in which a single play will at least tie the game

onside kick a short kickoff that can be recovered by either team

punt a kick that returns the ball to the other team

sacked tackled as a quarterback

two-minute warning a break called with two minutes left in each half

INDEX

READ MORE

Braun, Eric. *Making the Miracle: The Biggest Comebacks in Sports (Sports Illustrated Kids. Heroes and Heartbreakers).* North Mankato, MN: Capstone Press, 2023.

Buckley, James, Jr. *Who Is Tom Brady? (Official Who HQ).* New York: Penguin Workshop, 2021.

Hansen, Grace. *Tom Brady: NFL Great and Super Bowl MVP (History Maker Biographies).* Minneapolis: Abdo Kids, 2022.

LEARN MORE ONLINE

1. Go to **www.factsurfer.com** or scan the QR code below.
2. Enter **"Super Bowl Comeback"** into the search box.
3. Click on the cover of this book to see a list of websites.